Panini

First published in Great Britain in 2005 as *Great Grilled Sandwiches* by Hamlyn
This edition published in 2014 by Spruce
a division of Octopus Publishing Group Ltd,
Endeavour House, 189 Shaftesbury Avenue, London WC2H 8JY
www.octopusbooks.co.uk
www.octopusbooksusa.com

An Hachette UK Company www.hachette.co.uk

Distributed in the US by Hachette Book Group USA
237 Park Avenue, New York NY 10017 USA

Distributed in Canada by Canadian Manda Group
165 Dufferin Street, Toronto, Ontario, Canada M6K 3H6

Copyright © Octopus Publishing Group Ltd 2014

ISBN 978 1 84601 480 2
A CIP catalogue record for this book is available from the British Library
Printed and bound in China

1 2 3 4 5 6 7 8 9 10

Consultant Publisher Sarah Ford
Design Eoghan O'Brien and Michelle Tilly
Photographer Lis Parsons
Home Economist Emma Jane Frost
Stylist Rachel Jukes
Production Controller Sarah Connelly

Notes

The American Egg Board advises that eggs should not be consumed raw. This book contains some dishes made with raw or lightly cooked eggs. It is prudent for more vulnerable people, such as pregnant and nursing mothers, invalids, the elderly, babies, and young children, to avoid uncooked or lightly cooked dishes made with eggs.

Meat and poultry should be cooked thoroughly. To test if poultry is cooked, pierce the flesh through the thickest part with a skewer or fork—the juices should run clear, never pink or red. Keep refrigerated until ready for cooking.

This book includes dishes made with nuts and nut derivatives. It is advisable for those with known allergic reactions to nuts and nut derivatives and those who may potentially be vulnerable to these allergies, such as pregnant and nursing mothers, invalids, the elderly, babies, and children, to avoid dishes made with nuts and nut oils. It is also prudent to check the labels of pre-prepared ingredients for the possible inclusion of nut derivatives.

Panini

SENSATIONAL
GRILLED SANDWICHES

spruce

Contents

Introduction

TURN UP THE HEAT

These days sandwiches are seen as the quintessential lunchtime food. Quick to prepare, easy to eat, and filling, a sandwich can be eaten in a café, on the go, or even at your desk. The origins of the grilled sandwich can probably be traced to the Italian tradition of panini. Literally translated, *panino* means roll or sandwich, and that's basically what they are. But they are actually far more than that, incorporating as they do a real sense of the Italian attitude to food—occasion, enjoyment, and indulgence. Panini tend to eschew the more traditional sandwich fillings, elevating this popular morning snack and lunchtime fodder to greater heights, giving it a little more status.

The Italian attitude has spread, and now the grilled sandwich is usually regarded as something a little more refined than the ordinary, un-grilled sandwich. More unusual and expensive ingredients are often saved for this particular type of sandwich, which is really a way to enjoy a delicious meal without necessarily having to sit at a table and wait for something to be prepared.

BACK TO BASICS

The essential requirements for successful grilled sandwiches are good-quality ingredients, and the Italian attitude has fortunately accompanied this hot snack on its travels around the world. If the bread is wonderfully fresh and fragrant, one or two good fillings can be sufficient to create a delicious sandwich. In Italy, cured meats, such as speck and prosciutto, may be used alone or combined with a local cheese, which is selected because the flavors complement each other.

Grilling transforms a regular sandwich into something entirely different, changing the texture and taste of both the bread and the filling. Although there are a number of specific sandwich grills on the market these days, most cafés use a regular sandwich grill and, depending on the type of bread they use, they may weigh this down with a heavy object while the sandwich is toasting. This compacts the bread and helps to make sure that the filling is piping hot. It also ensures that the bread soaks up the delicious juices and flavors from the filling.

CHOOSING BREAD

Most types of bread can be used to make grilled sandwiches, but before you choose remember that the bread and filling have to undergo quite a tough cooking process, often being pressed down with some force for several minutes. You should always try to choose a sturdy bread that isn't going to collapse or break up in the grill. Homemade breads are fine to use, and other suitable choices include bagels (plain or flavored), sourdough bread, pita bread, English muffins, and croissants. The best way to find your favorite combinations is through trial and error.

The bread that you choose will have a huge impact on the final flavor of your sandwich, and some breads are better suited to particular fillings. The recipes in this book have been designed around the breads that they use, and there are ideas for every meal, including some unusual sweet sandwiches as well. For example, crêpes and panettone are ideal for sweet fillings, while baguettes and ciabatta are robust enough for strongly flavored ingredients. If you're using a highly textured or flavored bread, don't complicate it with too many competing flavors in the filling. It is important that every flavor is detectable and that the bread and filling work together to achieve an overall taste sensation.

THE RIGHT INGREDIENTS

There are, of course, many tried-and-true combinations that work especially well in grilled sandwiches, and you'll find many of these on the pages that follow.

Cheese

Because the sandwiches are grilled, some cheeses are perfect—fontina, haloumi, mozzarella, and goat cheese are just a few of the cheeses that take well to grilling. They melt gently and warm through, without losing their shape or becoming too runny.

Chicken

This is a good accompaniment for other complementary flavors, and it is delicious when served hot in a sandwich. Look out for the Thai Red Chicken on page 47, which is served with cashew satay sauce.

Ham

Cured ham works especially well in grilled sandwiches and was a traditional ingredient in the original Italian panini. The strong flavors are not overwhelmed by the bread that surrounds the meat or by the other ingredients that you use. Bacon is also a great sandwich filling, and can be combined with eggs to make a substantial breakfast.

Sauces

Use your favorite sauces with all types of sandwich fillings. Chutney, relish, flavored mayonnaise, and mustard can all be added to your sandwich, such as the use of mango chutney in the Crispy Camembert in naan bread on page 26, or you could try something different like harissa paste as in Herby Swordfish a la Plancha on page 29.

Vegetables

A wide range of vegetables can be used in grilled sandwiches, but bell peppers, zucchini, and onions are popular choices. Cook them quickly first if you want. Several recipes in this book are ideal for vegetarians, including more unusual ideas such as Brie, Peach, and Watercress (see page 21), and Roasted Chickpea and Tomato Salsa (see page 27).

TOP TIPS
FOR HOMEMADE
GRILLED SANDWICHES

Although practise makes perfect, there are a few guidelines that will help ensure that your grilled sandwiches turn out perfectly:

• Make sure all your ingredients are ready before you begin. Once you start assembling your sandwich, you don't want to be rushing around looking for half the ingredients. If bell peppers need to be grilled or chicken cooked, do it in advance. Consider using your sandwich grill to do so.

• Make sure your grill is hot enough to use before you put your sandwich on the plate. If you have a proper sandwich or panini grill, the light will indicate when it's hot enough to use. Be vigilant and lift the grill plate occasionally during cooking to check on your sandwiches—you don't want them sitting on a lukewarm grill or burning because you've left them to cook for too long.

• Don't pack too many ingredients into your sandwiches or they will spill out and burn on the grill. That doesn't mean you can't use a good selection of ingredients, but take care not to use too much of each. It will also be messy to eat if the filling is oozing out of it.

SPECIAL EQUIPMENT

• If you have a well-equipped kitchen, you shouldn't need to buy anything special to create gourmet snacks. A sandwich grill is essential if you're going to be making a lot of sandwiches, although it is possible to cook them in a ridged grill pan as long as you press down hard with a metal spatula. If you're a committed sandwich griller, you might want to invest in a panini press, a specially designed grill that can usually cook two sandwiches at once.

• You will need a spatula to remove your sandwiches from the grill so that they don't break up or lose any of the filling. Use a sharp knife to cut them in half before serving.

• Non-stick cooking spray is ideal for grilling sandwiches and is a healthier option than bottled oil. It gives a light coating of oil, which will prevent the bread from sticking to the grill, but it won't make the sandwiches greasy.

• So, with the pantry well stocked and the sandwich grill oiled and ready to use, the only thing remaining is for you to pick out your first recipe and start creating some wonderful grilled sandwiches. Be careful, however—once you start you may become addicted!

Glossary

US	UK
arugula	rocket
bacon slices	bacon rashers
bell pepper	sweet pepper
cilantro	fresh coriander
confectioners' sugar	icing sugar
ground beef	minced beef
heavy cream	double cream
peanut oil	groundnut oil
phyllo pastry	filo pastry
scallions	spring onions
shrimps	prawns
skillet	frying pan
superfine sugar	caster sugar
zucchini	courgette

Conversion Table

Standard American cup measurements are used in all recipes.

¼ cup = 60 ml (2 fl oz)
⅓ cup = 75 ml (3 fl oz)
½ cup = 120 ml (4 fl oz)
1 cup = 240 ml (8 fl oz)

TALEGGIO AND WILD MUSHROOMS

2 tablespoons butter
2 tablespoons olive oil
3 oz mixed wild mushrooms, trimmed
1 small garlic clove, chopped
2 tablespoons roughly chopped parsley
salt and pepper
2 large, all-butter croissants
3½ oz taleggio cheese, sliced

SOME SANDWICH GRILLS HAVE A "MELT" SETTING, WHICH MEANS THAT YOU CAN STOP THE TOP GRILL FROM COMING ALL THE WAY DOWN. THIS ENABLES YOU TO MAKE OPEN MELTED SANDWICHES, WHICH IS PERFECT FOR THIS RECIPE. IF YOUR MACHINE DOESN'T HAVE THIS SETTING, JUST PUT THE LIDS ON THE SANDWICHES AND COOK THEM LIKE REGULAR GRILLED SANDWICHES. ALTERNATIVELY, FINISH THEM OFF UNDER A HOT BROILER.

1. Melt the butter with the olive oil in a frying pan. Add the mushrooms, garlic, and parsley and fry over medium heat until soft and golden. Season well, remove from the heat, and allow to cool.

2. Split the croissants almost in half horizontally and top with the taleggio and sautéed wild mushrooms.

3. Set the sandwich grill to "melt," place the croissants on the bottom plate, and lower the top so that it stops just before it touches the cheese. Leave the machine to toast the bases of the croissants and gently melt the tops. Remove from the machine and serve immediately.

Gravlax

WITH CREAM CHEESE AND CHIVES

2 poppy and sesame seed bagels, cut in half
4 oz cream cheese
6 oz gravlax, thinly sliced
2 tablespoons snipped chives
freshly ground black pepper, plus extra to serve
warmed hollandaise sauce, to serve

1. Place the bagels, cut side down, on a sandwich grill. Without closing the lid, leave them to toast for 2–3 minutes until golden. Remove from the grill. Spread the bases with the cream cheese and top with the gravlax. Scatter the snipped chives over the bagel and season with black pepper.

2. Top with the lids and return to the sandwich grill. Lower the top plate and toast for 2–3 minutes, or according to the manufacturer's instructions, until golden and crispy. Serve immediately with warmed hollandaise sauce and more black pepper.

Brunch CROQUE MONSIEUR

BRING A LITTLE TASTE OF FRANCE TO YOUR BRUNCH TABLE WITH THIS BISTRO FAVORITE. THE GRATED PARMESAN COATING GIVES THE TOAST AN IRRESISTIBLE CRUNCH. TRY TOPPING WITH A PERFECT FRIED EGG TO MAKE A CROQUE MADAME.

4 thick slices of French country bread
2 tablespoons melted butter
¼ cup finely grated Parmesan cheese
2 large slices of country-style roast ham
1 cup Emmental or similar Swiss cheese, grated
fried egg (optional, for croque madame)

1. Brush one side of each slice of country bread with the melted butter using a pastry brush and sprinkle with the Parmesan. Making sure that the Parmesan coated sides are on the outside, lay down 2 slices of bread and top each with a slice of ham and half the coarsely grated Emmental.

2. Top with the other slices of bread and toast in a sandwich grill for 4–5 minutes, or according to the manufacturer's instructions, until the bread is golden and crispy and the cheese is beginning to ooze from the sides.

3. Serve immediately. Top the sandwich with a fried egg if you wish to make it into a brunch croque madame.

Spanish Frittata

THE SUN IS SHINING AND SUMMER IS JUST AROUND THE CORNER. THIS SANDWICH IS FOR THOSE LONG, LAZY SUNDAY BREAKFASTS THAT LAST UNTIL LUNCHTIME.

¼ cup olive oil
1 small red onion, halved and cut into strips
4 oz cold, cooked potatoes, thickly sliced
2 oz thinly sliced chorizo sausage, shredded (optional)
3 oz roasted red bell peppers, cut into strips
1 garlic clove, crushed
½ teaspoon paprika
¼ cup roughly chopped flat leaf parsley
2 teaspoons chopped marjoram
3 large eggs, lightly beaten
salt and pepper
½ cup grated Cheddar cheese
4 slices of multigrain bread

1. Heat the olive oil in a small frying pan. Add the onion and fry over medium heat until it is softened and golden. Add the potatoes and fry until they are hot and golden. Add the chorizo (if using), bell peppers, garlic, paprika, and herbs, and stir with a spatula. Add the eggs and some seasoning and allow the mixture to cook until the eggs set, stirring once to prevent the mixture from sticking.

2. Scatter the Cheddar over the frittata and place the frying pan under a preheated broiler until the cheese is melted and bubbling. Remove and leave to cool. Once the frittata is cool enough to handle, cut it into thick wedges and place each wedge on a slice of multigrain bread. Top with the remaining two slices to form two sandwiches and toast in a sandwich grill for 2–3 minutes, or according to the manufacturer's instructions, until the bread is golden and crispy. Serve immediately.

OAT & APPLE
FRUESLI

A PERFECT START TO YOUR MORNING, THIS WHOLESOME BREAKFAST ALTERNATIVE WILL LEAVE YOU FEELING VIRTUOUS ALL DAY LONG!

¼ cup rolled oats
¼ cup rolled wheat flakes
2 tablespoons sunflower seeds
2 tablespoons sweetened puffed quinoa
1 dried, chopped, ready-to-eat banana
2 dried, chopped, ready-to-eat apricots
5 slices crisp, dried apple, crumbled
¼ cup golden raisins
2 tablespoons dried, shaved coconut (optional)
2 tablespoons light brown sugar
¼ cup apple juice
¼ cup Greek yogurt
4 large slices of cinnamon raisin bread
Greek yogurt, to serve

1. Mix together all the dry ingredients in a bowl and stir in the apple juice and yogurt until well coated. Spoon onto 2 slices of cinnamon raisin bread and place the remaining 2 slices on top.

2. Toast in a sandwich grill for 2–3 minutes, or according to the manufacturer's instructions, until crisp and golden. Serve immediately with an extra bowl of Greek yogurt and a glass of apple juice.

Ricotta
AND PEAR
DRIZZLE

WHETHER YOU ARE PLANNING A LAZY DAY OR ARE IN THE MOOD FOR A SPECIAL TREAT, THIS MOUTH-WATERING BREAKFAST COMBINATION IS PERFECTION ITSELF.

½ cup ricotta cheese
4 thick slices of all-butter brioche
1 small, sweet dessert pear, cored and thinly sliced
¼ cup runny honey, plus extra for drizzling

1. Spread the ricotta thickly over 2 slices of brioche and fan out the pear slices over the top. Drizzle with the honey and top with the remaining slices of brioche.

2. Toast in a sandwich grill for 1–2 minutes, or according to the manufacturer's instructions, until the bread is crisp and golden. Cut in half diagonally and serve immediately, drizzled with extra honey.

GRILLED SWEET POTATO AND BLUE CHEESE

POTATO CAKES ARE A TRADITIONAL IRISH FOOD AND ARE AVAILABLE IN SUPERMARKETS AND IRISH SPECIALIST FOOD STORES. IF YOU CAN'T FIND POTATO CAKES, PITA BREAD MAKES A GOOD SUBSTITUTE IN THIS RECIPE.

¼ cup honey
1 teaspoon crushed red pepper flakes
¼ cup sesame oil
½ cup olive oil
1 large sweet potato, thickly sliced
½ cup sugar-snap peas
2 potato cakes
2 oz blue cheese, such as Roquefort
salt and freshly ground black pepper

1. Combine the honey, red pepper flakes, sesame oil, and olive oil in a small bowl. Place the sweet potato slices and sugar-snap peas in a large bowl and toss them with half of the honey dressing until they are evenly coated. Season well and place on a baking sheet, arranging the vegetables so that the potatoes are in a single layer. Place them under a hot broiler for 8 minutes, turning occasionally with tongs until the potatoes are soft and turning golden.

2. When they are cool enough to handle, arrange the potato slices and peas over half the base of each potato cake and crumble the blue cheese over them. Fold the potato cakes to create two sandwiches and toast in a sandwich grill for 3–4 minutes, or according to the manufacturer's instructions, until the bread is golden and the cheese is just melting. Serve immediately with a small bowl of the remaining honey dressing to drizzle.

VEGETARIAN
QUESADILLA

¼ cup refried beans
4 taco-size tortillas
1 cup cooked long-grain white rice
1 red bell pepper, thinly sliced
1 onion, thinly sliced
⅔ cup pinto beans, cooked and drained
¼ cup salsa
1 large tomato, seeded and sliced
2 jalapeño peppers, sliced (optional)
3 oz Monterey Jack cheese, sliced

To serve
sour cream
guacamole

1. Spread the refried beans over half of each tortilla and spoon the cooked rice over them. Scatter with the red bell pepper and onion and then the pinto beans. Spoon on the salsa and top with the tomato and jalapeño peppers (if using), and finish with the sliced Monterey Jack.

2. Fold the tortillas in half and toast in a sandwich grill for 3–4 minutes, or according to the manufacturer's instructions, until the tortillas are crispy and the filling is hot and melted. Serve immediately with sour cream and guacamole.

LEMON MOZZARELLA AND PARMESAN

4 slices of poppy seed bread
½ cup finely grated Parmesan cheese
2 tablespoons capers, rinsed
¼ cup pine nuts, lightly toasted
finely grated zest of 1 lemon
4 oz mozzarella cheese, sliced
handful of arugula leaves
2 tablespoons lemon juice
salt and freshly ground black pepper

1. Sprinkle 2 slices of poppy seed bread with half the Parmesan and scatter the capers, pine nuts, and lemon zest over the cheese. Arrange the mozzarella slices on top and scatter the arugula leaves over them. Drizzle with lemon juice, season well, and sprinkle with the remaining Parmesan.

2. Top with the lids and toast in a sandwich grill for 2–3 minutes, or according to the manufacturer's instructions, until the bread is toasted and the melted mozzarella is oozing from the sides.

Brie Peach, AND WATERCRESS

3½ oz firm Brie, sliced
1 small baguette, cut in half and sliced horizontally
1 peach, pitted and sliced
1 small bunch of watercress
freshly ground black pepper
2 tablespoons olive oil

1. Arrange the sliced Brie over the bases of the baguette halves and top with the peach slices. Scatter the watercress leaves over the peaches and grind black pepper over them. Drizzle with olive oil and top with the lids.

2. Toast in a sandwich grill for 2–3 minutes, or according to the manufacturer's instructions, until the bread is crispy and the cheese is beginning to ooze. Serve immediately.

ROASTED
RED PEPPER AND FETA

2 red Romano peppers, halved lengthwise, and seeded
3 oz feta cheese, sliced
1 teaspoon dried oregano
1 teaspoon finely grated lemon zest
¼ cup olive oil
2 tablespoons balsamic vinegar
2 tablespoons pesto sauce
2 pieces of foccacia, cut in half horizontally
small handful of red chard leaves
salt and freshly ground black pepper

1. Place the peppers cut side up in a roasting pan and place the feta slices inside each half. Scatter with the oregano and lemon zest and season well. Drizzle with the olive oil and balsamic vinegar and cook in a preheated 350° oven for 25–30 minutes, until the peppers are softened and starting to blacken around the edges. Remove and set aside to cool.

2. Spread the pesto over the bases of the foccacia and arrange the chard leaves on top. Layer the peppers over the chard and top with the lids. Toast in a sandwich grill for 3–4 minutes, or according to the manufacturer's instructions, until the bread is golden and the leaves are wilted.

Potato and
ONION BLINIS

½ cup olive oil
1 small red onion, thinly sliced
2½ cups grated potato
pinch of dried thyme
4 large blinis
¼ cup mascarpone cheese, plus extra to serve
¼ cup oil-cured, pitted black olives, halved
salt and freshly ground black pepper

1. Heat the olive oil in a large frying pan over a medium heat. Add the onion and grated potato and fry gently for 10 minutes, turning frequently, until golden and crispy. Stir in the thyme, season well, and remove from the heat.

2. Spread the bases of 2 blinis with the mascarpone and carefully spoon the potato mixture over it. Scatter with the olives and cover with the remaining 2 blinis.

3. Toast the blinis in a sandwich grill for 2–3 minutes, or according to the manufacturer's instructions, until they are golden and crispy and the filling is hot. Serve immediately with extra mascarpone.

CRISPY
CAMEMBERT

THE COMBINATION OF THE SWEET INDIAN BREAD AND FRUITY MANGO CHUTNEY CUTS THROUGH THE RICHNESS OF THE CAMEMBERT IN THIS TASTY RECIPE.

⅓ cup fresh breadcrumbs
2 tablespoons chopped chervil
1 teaspoon finely grated lemon zest
salt and freshly ground black pepper
4 oz Camembert cheese, thickly sliced
¼ cup vegetable oil
¼ cup fruity mango chutney
2 small peshwari naan breads, cut in half horizontally
1 scallion, sliced

1. Combine the breadcrumbs, chervil, and lemon zest in a bowl with some salt and pepper. Empty onto a plate and press the Camembert slices into the breadcrumb mix, making sure they are thoroughly coated.

2. Heat the oil in a small frying pan and fry the cheese for 3–4 minutes until golden and crispy. Remove from the pan and drain any excess oil on paper towels. Spread the mango chutney over the bases of the peshwari naan breads and scatter the sliced scallion over it. Arrange the crispy Camembert over the onion and top with the lids.

3. Toast in a sandwich grill for 2 minutes, or according to the manufacturer's instructions, until the bread is hot and crispy. Cut in half and serve immediately.

ROASTED CHICKPEA
AND TOMATO SALSA

2 garlic and herb naan breads, cut in half horizontally

Salsa
1 x 14-oz can chickpeas, drained and rinsed
¼ cup olive oil
1 teaspoon cumin seeds, toasted
½ teaspoon smoked paprika
2 plum tomatoes, seeded and chopped
1 small red onion, halved and thinly sliced
1 garlic clove, chopped
¾-inch cube fresh root ginger, peeled and finely shredded
salt and freshly ground black pepper

THIS RECIPE CONTAINS A DELICIOUS SMOKY CHICKPEA AND TOMATO SALSA, FULL OF GARLICKY GINGER FLAVORS, WHICH IS ROASTED BEFORE BEING USED AS A FILLING FOR AN IRRESISTIBLE TOASTED SANDWICH.

1. Toss the salsa ingredients together and place them in a large roasting pan. Cook in a preheated 425° oven for 25 minutes, until the salsa is sticky and golden.

2. Remove the salsa from the oven and spoon onto the bases of the naan breads. Top with the lids and toast in a sandwich grill for 2–3 minutes, or according to the manufacturer's instructions, until the bread is golden and crispy. Cut into wedges and serve immediately.

Herby Swordfish
A LA PLANCHA

2 swordfish steaks, about 6 oz each
2 tablespoons olive oil
2 tablespoons chopped oregano
2 teaspoons chopped thyme
finely grated zest of 1 lemon
salt and freshly ground black pepper
2 tablespoons pine nuts, lightly toasted
2 tablespoons capers, rinsed
2 sun-dried tomato ciabatta rolls, cut in half
2 teaspoons harissa paste
large handful of arugula leaves

THE TERM *A LA PLANCHA* IS USED TO DESCRIBE SOMETHING THAT IS COOKED ON A GRIDDLE, BUT IN THIS RECIPE IT IS THE PLATES OF THE SANDWICH GRILL THAT FIRST COOK THE SWORDFISH, AND THEN THE SANDWICH ITSELF, SHOWING HOW VERSATILE THE SANDWICH GRILL CAN BE.

1. Rub the swordfish steaks with the olive oil, chopped herbs, and grated lemon zest, then season well with salt and pepper.

2. Heat the sandwich grill and place the swordfish inside, bringing down the top plate. Cook for about 2 minutes and then remove the fish. Wipe the machine with a damp cloth.

3. Scatter the pine nuts and capers over the base of each ciabatta roll. Lay the swordfish steaks on top, then spread a thin layer of harissa on the lids and place them on top of the sandwiches.

4. Toast the sandwiches in the clean sandwich grill for about 4 minutes, or according to the manufacturer's instructions, until the bread is hot. Remove from the sandwich grill and add the arugula leaves. Serve immediately.

Miso Tuna
AND WILTED GREENS

2 tuna steaks, about 6 oz each
¼ cup miso soup paste
1 head of bok choy, halved
2 pita breads, cut in half horizontally
large handful of baby spinach leaves
1 teaspoon sesame oil

1. Rub the tuna steaks all over with the miso soup paste and set aside for at least 20 minutes to marinate. Preheat a frying pan and cook the tuna for 3–4 minutes, turning once, until almost cooked. Add the halves of bok choy, cut side down, for the last 2 minutes of cooking time.

2. Remove both the tuna and the bok choy and arrange them on the bases of the pita breads. Toss the spinach leaves in the sesame oil and place on top of the tuna. Top with the lids then toast in a sandwich grill for 1–2 minutes, or according to the manufacturer's instructions, until the bread is crispy and the spinach has wilted.

Breaded Hake
AND CRUSHED PEAS

1 cup frozen petite peas
2 tablespoons butter
salt and freshly ground black pepper
¼ cup finely chopped mint
¼ cup fresh breadcrumbs
finely grated zest of 1 lemon
¼ cup chopped parsley
1 large egg, lightly beaten
2 hake fillets, about 4 oz each
⅓ cup vegetable oil
2 large, soft, floured rolls, cut in half horizontally
tartar sauce, to serve

1. Bring a pan of salted water to a rolling boil and cook the peas for about 4 minutes until they are soft. Drain and return to the pan with the butter and some salt and pepper. Use a potato masher to crush the peas so that they are almost puréed. Stir in the chopped mint and set aside.

2. Mix the breadcrumbs with the lemon zest, some salt and pepper, and the chopped parsley, and spread on a large plate. Pour the beaten egg into a shallow bowl and dip the hake fillets into it before placing them on the breadcrumbs. Turn the fish in the breadcrumbs, making sure that the flesh is completely covered.

3. Heat the oil in a medium-sized frying pan and lay the fish in the pan over a medium-high heat. Cook the fish for about 4 minutes, turning once, until it is cooked through and the breadcrumbs are golden and crispy.

4. Spread the crushed peas over the bases of the rolls and lay the fish on top. Top with the lids then toast in a sandwich grill for 2–3 minutes, or according to the manufacturer's instructions, until the bread is golden and crispy. Cut each sandwich into quarters and serve with tartar sauce.

TERIYAKI SALMON
WITH WASABI DRESSING

2 salmon fillets, about 6 oz each
2 large sesame seed buns, cut in half horizontally
1 scallion, finely sliced
finely shredded cucumber, to serve

Teriyaki sauce
¼ cup soy sauce
½ cup sake
½ cup mirin
2 tablespoons light brown sugar
½-inch cube fresh root ginger, peeled and finely shredded
1 garlic clove, chopped

Wasabi dressing
1 teaspoon sesame oil
1 teaspoon wasabi paste
2 tablespoons superfine sugar
2 teaspoons soy sauce
⅓ cup rice wine vinegar

IF YOU'RE SHORT ON TIME, YOU CAN ALWAYS BUY READY-MADE TERIYAKI SAUCE, BUT THIS RECIPE IS EASY AND KEEPS FOR SEVERAL WEEKS IN THE REFRIGERATOR.

1. Make the teriyaki sauce. Place all the ingredients in a small pan and heat gently until the sugar dissolves. Remove from the heat. Once the sauce is cold, place the salmon fillets in a shallow dish with the sauce and leave to marinate for 30 minutes to 1 hour.

2. Transfer the salmon fillets and teriyaki sauce into a heated frying pan and cook the fillets over medium heat, basting frequently with the sauce, for 2–3 minutes each side, or until they are almost cooked.

3. Lift the salmon onto the sesame seed bun bases. Top with the lids and toast in a sandwich grill for 2–3 minutes, or according to the manufacturer's instructions, until the bread is golden and crispy. Remove from the sandwich grill and cut each sandwich in half, then each half into canapé-sized pieces.

4. Combine the wasabi dressing ingredients in a screw-top jar. Pour the dressing into little dishes and sprinkle with the sliced scallion. Serve immediately with the salmon sandwiches and shredded cucumber.

CRISPY SEAWEED AND
Shrimp

oil, for shallow frying
6 sheets dried nori seaweed, finely shredded
7 oz cooked shrimp
½ teaspoon crushed red pepper flakes (optional)
2 tablespoons toasted sesame seeds
2 tablespoons chili oil
½-inch cube fresh root ginger, peeled and finely sliced
4 taco-size tortillas
soy sauce, to serve

1. Heat the oil in a deep frying pan to 350° or until a cube of bread browns in 20 seconds. Carefully drop the seaweed into the oil for a few seconds, scooping it out with a large slotted spoon as soon as it goes crispy. Drain on plenty of paper towels to get rid of excess oil and set aside.

2. In a bowl toss together the shrimp, red pepper flakes (if using), sesame seeds, chili oil, and shredded ginger. Place the mixture on the tortillas, covering half of each one, and fold over the other half to enclose the shrimp mixture.

3. Toast in a sandwich grill for 2–3 minutes, or according to the manufacturer's instructions, until hot and crispy. Cut each tortilla crescent into 3 equal pieces and serve immediately with the crispy seaweed and a small bowl of soy sauce.

CILANTRO AND CHILI CRAB

PHYLLO PASTRY WORKS WONDERFULLY TO MAKE THIS ZINGY CRAB PARCEL.

4 phyllo pastry sheets, about 8 x 12 inches each
¼ cup melted butter

Crab filling
1 lemon grass stalk
1 x 6-oz can crab meat, drained
finely grated zest of 1 lime
2 tablespoons chopped cilantro leaves
2 tablespoons chopped cilantro roots
2 tablespoons chopped mint
2 tablespoons lime juice
1 small red chile, seeded and finely chopped
2 tablespoons fish sauce
½ teaspoon palm sugar
salt and freshly ground black pepper

1. Strip the lemon grass stalk of its outer layers and finely slice the soft heart. Mix it in a bowl together with all the remaining crab filling ingredients, season, and set aside.

2. Brush each sheet of phyllo pastry with melted butter and arrange 2 of them crosswise over each other. Repeat with the remaining 2 sheets.

3. Spoon the crab mixture into the middle of each pastry arrangement and fold over the sides to create neat parcels.

4. Toast in a sandwich grill for 3–4 minutes, or according to the manufacturer's instructions, until the pastry is golden and crispy. Serve immediately.

Super Club

WITH GRAIN MUSTARD

¼ cup mayonnaise, plus extra to serve
2 tablespoons wholegrain mustard, plus extra to serve
4 slices of multigrain bread
2 slices of honey-roast ham
3 oz deli-style turkey, in wafer-thin slices
3 oz sharp Cheddar cheese, thinly sliced
1 large beefsteak tomato, sliced
½ small red onion, thinly sliced
6 slices of cooked, smoked bacon
6 cornichons, finely sliced (optional)
freshly chopped chives

1. Combine the mayonnaise and mustard in a small bowl and spread the mixture over 1 side of each slice of multigrain bread. Arrange the ham slices on 2 slices of bread, followed by the sliced turkey. Top with half of the Cheddar, then the tomato and the red onion. Next, top with the bacon and cornichon slices (if using), then the remainder of the cheese; sprinkle the chives over the filling before covering with the remaining 2 slices of bread.

2. Toast in a sandwich grill for 3–4 minutes, or according to the manufacturer's instructions, until the filling is hot and melting and the bread is golden. Serve immediately with extra mayonnaise and mustard sauce and plenty of napkins!

Pastrami

WITH RED ONION CHUTNEY

4 slices of rye bread
5 oz shaved pastrami
2 slices of sharp Cheddar cheese
barbecue sauce, to serve

Red onion chutney
2 tablespoons butter
2 tablespoons chili oil
2 red onions, sliced
1 teaspoon black mustard seeds
2 tablespoons sherry vinegar
salt and freshly ground black pepper

1. Make the chutney. Heat the butter and chili oil in a frying pan and add the onions and mustard seeds. Fry gently over a low heat for about 15 minutes until the onions are soft and lightly golden in color. Stir in the sherry vinegar, season well, and set aside to cool.

2. Spoon the onion chutney onto 2 slices of rye bread and layer the shaved pastrami on top. Place the slices of Cheddar on the pastrami and top with the lids. Toast in a sandwich grill for 3–4 minutes, or according to the manufacturer's instructions, until the bread is toasted and the cheese has melted. Serve immediately with barbecue sauce.

PHILLY CHEESE STEAK

¼ cup olive oil
½ red bell pepper, cored and thinly sliced
½ green bell pepper, cored and thinly sliced
1 small onion, halved and thinly sliced
10 oz rib-eye steak, thinly sliced
1 cup mushrooms, trimmed and sliced
1 garlic clove, chopped
3 oz provolone cheese, thinly sliced
2 tablespoons Worcestershire or steak sauce
4 long slices of French country bread
1 dill pickle, thinly sliced (optional)
salt and freshly ground black pepper

To serve
2 tablespoons barbeque sauce
cherry tomatoes

1. Heat the olive oil in a frying pan and add the peppers and onion. Cook over a medium-high heat for 3–4 minutes until they just begin to soften. Add the steak and continue cooking for 2–3 minutes before adding the mushrooms and garlic. Cook for a further 3–4 minutes.

2. Reduce the heat to low, season well, and then use 2 wooden spatulas to form the steak mixture into 2 piles, roughly the size of the bread slices. Place the slices of cheese on top of each pile and leave to melt for 2 minutes.

3. Spread a little of the Worcestershire or steak sauce over 2 slices of bread and then very carefully lift the cheese-steak mixture onto the French country bread, again using 2 spatulas. Splash the remaining sauce over the mixture and arrange the pickle slices on top (if using).

4. Top with the 2 remaining bread slices to form 2 sandwiches and toast in a sandwich grill for 2–3 minutes, or according to the manufacturer's instructions, until the bread is crispy and the cheese is completely melted. Serve immediately with barbeque sauce and a bowl of cherry tomatoes.

SMOKY BACON,
TOMATO, AND AVOCADO

TRY THIS AS A DELICIOUSLY DIFFERENT ALTERNATIVE TO A BLT. THE COMBINATION OF THE CREAMY AVOCADO WITH CRISPY BACON IS A REAL LUNCHTIME TREAT.

4 oz mozzarella cheese, sliced
4 slices of Irish soda bread
4 slices of cooked Irish-style bacon
1 small avocado, peeled, pitted and sliced
8 cherry tomatoes, halved
2 scallions, thinly sliced
2 tablespoons basil oil
freshly ground black pepper

1. Arrange the mozzarella slices over 2 slices of soda bread. Top with the bacon, avocado, and halved cherry tomatoes. Sprinkle with the sliced scallions and drizzle with basil oil. Season well with freshly ground black pepper and top with the remaining bread.

2. Toast the sandwiches in a sandwich grill for 3–4 minutes, or according to the manufacturer's instructions, until the bread is golden and the cheese is melting.

Pork
TENDERLION
MEDALLIONS WITH APPLE

⅓ cup olive oil
10 oz pork tenderloin, thinly sliced
¼ cup cider vinegar
¼ cup hard cider
2 shallots, finely chopped
2 teaspoons chopped thyme
1 bay leaf
⅓ cup crème fraîche
2 tablespoons butter
1 apple, cored and sliced
7 oz readymade rolled puff pastry
salt and freshly ground black pepper
arugula, to garnish

1. Heat ¼ cup of the olive oil in a large frying pan and fry the pork slices until golden. Pour in half the cider and the cider vinegar and heat until the liquid bubbles and evaporates. Remove the pork from the pan and set aside. Wipe the pan with a paper towel and add 1 teaspoon of the olive oil. Fry the shallots in the pan gently until soft and golden. Add 1 teaspoon of the thyme, the bay leaf, crème fraîche, and the remaining cider, and season. Reserve the sauce and keep warm.

2. In a separate frying pan, heat the butter and the remaining olive oil. Add the apple slices and fry over a medium high heat until golden and caramelized. Remove with a slotted spoon and drain on paper towels.

3. Cut the pastry into 2 x 6-inch squares. Imagine there is a diagonal line through the pastry squares and arrange the apple and pork slices over one side of the line, sprinkle with the remaining thyme, season well, and fold to form two triangular parcels. Toast in a sandwich grill for 5–6 minutes, or according to the manufacturer's instructions, until the pastry is golden and crisp. Serve immediately with the reserved sauce and arugula garnish.

BLACK FOREST
HAM, CHEESE,
AND ASPARAGUS

STEAM THE ASPARAGUS SO THAT IT IS *AL DENTE* AND STILL FIRM—THE SLIGHT CRUNCH CONTRASTS WONDERFULLY WITH THE OOZING MELTED CHEESE.

4 thin slices of Black Forest ham
3 oz fontina cheese, grated
small handful of arugula
4 oz bundle of trimmed asparagus spears, steamed
2 vine-ripened tomatoes, sliced
4 slices of sourdough bread
2 tablespoons olive oil
2 teaspoons balsamic vinegar

1. Arrange the ham, grated fontina, arugula, asparagus, and tomatoes over 2 slices of sourdough bread. Drizzle with the olive oil and balsamic vinegar and top with the lids.

2. Toast the sandwiches in a sandwich grill for 3–4 minutes, or according to the manufacturer's instructions, until the bread is golden and the cheese has melted. Serve immediately.

R O A S T E D
ROSEMARY
CHICKEN

2 chicken breasts, about 5 oz each
2 teaspoons tapenade
4 sun-dried tomatoes
1 garlic clove, cut into slivers
3–4 sprigs of rosemary
2 tablespoons olive oil
salt and freshly ground black pepper
2 large wholegrain rolls, cut in half horizontally
2 oz pecorino cheese, shaved
arugula, to garnish

1. Using a sharp knife, make a horizontal slit in each chicken breast. Do not cut all the way through but just deep enough to create a pocket in the flesh. Stuff the tapenade, sun-dried tomatoes, and garlic slivers into the pocket and close it up. Lay the chicken breasts on top of the rosemary sprigs in a roasting pan and drizzle with olive oil. Season with a little salt and pepper and cook in a preheated 350° oven for about 18 minutes, until the chicken is cooked through.

2. When the chicken is cool enough to handle, cut it into slices. Arrange the meat on the wholegrain roll bases, sprinkle with the pecorino shavings, and top with the lids. Toast in a sandwich grill for 3–4 minutes, or according to the manufacturer's instructions, until the bread is golden and the chicken is hot. Serve immediately garnished with arugula.

Chicken Caesar

2 tablespoons olive oil
4 slices of bacon
4 oz cooked chicken breast, sliced
1 small wholegrain baguette, cut in half horizontally
$1/3$ cup ready-made Caesar dressing, plus extra to serve
4 anchovies in olive oil, drained (optional)
1 oz Parmesan cheese, shaved
Bibb or other butter lettuce, to serve

1. Heat a small frying pan over a medium heat and add the olive oil. Place the bacon in the pan and fry for 2–3 minutes, turning once, until crisp and golden.

2. Layer the slices of chicken breast on the base of the wholegrain baguette and top with the bacon. Drizzle with the Caesar dressing and top with the anchovies (if using) and the Parmesan shavings.

3. Put the top of the baguette over the filling, slice into two equal halves, and place in a sandwich grill. Toast for 5–6 minutes, or according to the manufacturer's instructions, until the sandwiches are hot throughout and golden and crispy.

4. Serve the sandwiches immediately together with the lettuce and some extra Caesar dressing for drizzling.

THAI RED CHICKEN

LEFTOVER SATAY SAUCE CAN BE KEPT FOR AT LEAST A WEEK IN A SCREW-TOP JAR IN THE REFRIGERATOR—BUT IT MAY BE TOO DELICIOUS TO LAST!

10 oz boneless chicken thighs, thickly sliced
⅓ cup Thai red curry paste
2 pita breads, split in half horizontally

Satay sauce
1 cup cashew nuts, lightly toasted
1 teaspoon crushed red pepper flakes
¼ cup soy sauce
1 cup coconut milk
¼ cup cilantro leaves
2 tablespoons palm sugar or light brown sugar
2 tablespoons rice wine vinegar
2 kaffir lime leaves, shredded
2 tablespoons peanut oil

1. To make the sauce, place the nuts in a food processor and pulse until finely chopped. Place in a small pan with the remaining satay ingredients and heat gently for 4–5 minutes, stirring frequently to prevent sticking, until the sauce is thick and glossy.

2. Coat the chicken thighs with the red curry paste and thread on to 4 metal skewers. Preheat the sandwich grill and lay the skewers directly on the heat, bringing down the top plate to seal the chicken. Grill for 4–5 minutes, until the chicken is thoroughly cooked. Set aside to cool. Push the chicken off the skewers directly into the pita breads. Toast the breads in the cleaned sandwich grill for 1–2 minutes, or according to the manufacturer's instructions, until they are crispy and the chicken is hot. Cut each pita in half and serve with a bowl of the warm cashew satay sauce.

TURKEY AND
CRANBERRY SAUCE

ENJOY THE TASTE OF THANKSGIVING ANYTIME WITH THIS TASTY GRILLED SANDWICH—YOU COULD EVEN USE TURKEY LEFTOVERS. A GOOD QUALITY CRANBERRY SAUCE IS ESSENTIAL.

⅓ cup cranberry sauce (made from whole berries)
4 slices of corn bread
¾ cup corn kernels
4 oz smoked turkey breast, thinly sliced

1. Spread the cranberry sauce over 2 slices of corn bread. Scatter the corn kernels over it, then top with the smoked turkey.

2. Top with the lids and toast in a sandwich grill for 2–3 minutes, or according to the manufacturer's instructions, until the bread is golden and crispy.

SLICED DUCK
BREAST

IF YOUR FAVORITE ITEM ON THE MENU OF YOUR LOCAL CHINESE RESTAURANT IS THE CRISPY DUCK PANCAKE, YOU ARE SURE TO LOVE THIS RECIPE. BRINGING THE TAKEOUT TO YOU!

¼ cup honey
¼ cup dark soy sauce
1 teaspoon five spice powder
2 duck breasts, about 5 oz each
¼ cup hoisin sauce, plus extra to serve
4 taco-size tortillas
2 scallions, sliced lengthwise
sliced cucumber, to serve

1. In a small bowl mix together the honey, soy sauce, and five spice powder. Use a sharp knife to make 3–4 cuts in each duck breast and rub the honey mixture generously all over the meat, making sure it gets into each cut.

2. Heat the sandwich grill and place the duck breasts inside, pushing the top plate down heavily. Leave to cook for 5–6 minutes, until the outside is crispy and golden and the inside is almost cooked. Remove from the grill and set aside to cool. Wipe the machine with a damp cloth.

3. Use a sharp knife to slice the duck breasts thinly. Spread a little hoisin sauce over the base of each tortilla. Arrange the duck on the sauce over half of each tortilla base and then scatter the sliced scallions over it.

4. Fold the tortillas in half and toast in the sandwich grill for 2–3 minutes or according to the manufacturer's instructions, until they are golden and crispy. Serve immediately with cucumber slices and extra hoisin sauce.

MELTING
ICE CREAM AND RASPBERRIES

1 cup raspberries
finely grated zest of 1 orange
2 tablespoons orange juice
2 tablespoons kirsch
2 tablespoons orange blossom honey
2 large English tea cakes, or sweet bagels, cut in half
2 large scoops vanilla-raspberry swirl ice cream

1. In a large bowl toss together the raspberries, grated orange zest and juice, kirsch, and orange blossom honey.

2. Spoon the raspberry mixture onto the tea cake or bagel bases, top with the lids, and toast in a sandwich grill for 2–3 minutes, or according to the manufacturer's instructions, until golden and crispy.

3. Cut each grilled sandwich into thin slices. Serve immediately with a scoop of vanilla-raspberry swirl ice cream.

Chocolate, GINGER, AND BANANA PARCELS

4 sheets phyllo pastry, each 8 x 12 inches
¼ cup melted butter
1 large banana, sliced lengthwise
3 oz dark chocolate, chopped
½ cup pecan nut halves, roughly chopped
¼ cup dark brown sugar
½ teaspoon ground ginger
pinch of apple-pie spice
vanilla ice cream, to serve

IF YOU ARE IN THE MOOD FOR COMFORT FOOD, LOOK NO FURTHER!

1. Brush the sheets of phyllo with the melted butter and arrange them in 2 stacks of 2 sheets. Arrange slices of banana in the middle of each stack, scatter with the chopped chocolate and pecans, and sprinkle with the sugar and spices.

2. Fold over the sides of the phyllo pastry to form 2 parcels and toast in a sandwich grill for 3–4 minutes, or according to the manufacturer's instructions, until the pastry is crisp and golden. Serve hot, with a scoop of vanilla ice cream.

Lemon
CREAM
AND CRUNCHY
HONEYCOMB

THIS IS A LOVELY, FRESH, SUMMERY DESSERT—WONDERFUL ENJOYED WITH A CHILLED GLASS OF HOMEMADE LEMONADE.

¼ cup heavy cream, plus extra to serve
1½ oz honeycomb or old-fashioned cinder toffee, crumbled
1 teaspoon finely grated lemon zest
¼ cup candied lemon peel, finely chopped (optional)
⅓ cup traditional lemon curd
6 Scotch pancakes
blueberries, to serve

1. In a bowl combine the cream, honeycomb, lemon zest, candied peel (if using), and lemon curd. Place a dollop of the lemon cream on a pancake, top with a second pancake and another dollop of lemon cream on top then finish with a third pancake. Repeat the process so that you are left with 2 triple-decker lemon pancakes.

2. Toast the pancake stacks in a sandwich grill for 1–2 minutes, or according to the manufacturer's instructions, until the outer pancakes are toasted and the lemon cream is beginning the ooze from the sides. Serve immediately with some blueberries.

Mango and Mint
WITH WARM BLACKBERRY COULIS

1½ cups blackberries
⅓ cup superfine sugar
2 tablespoons cassis liqueur (at least 16% alcohol)
4 thick slices of all-butter brioche
1 small, ripe mango, pitted, peeled and thinly sliced
6–8 small mint leaves, shredded

To serve
crème fraîche
2 sprigs of mint
confectioners' sugar

1. In a small pan gently warm 1 cup of the blackberries with ¼ cup of the sugar and 2 tablespoons of cold water until the sugar dissolves completely. Allow the mixture to bubble gently so the blackberries collapse, creating a thick fruity liquid. Remove from the heat and leave to cool. Use a blender to purée into a rich, smooth coulis, stir in the cassis, and set aside.

2. Sprinkle 1 tablespoon of the remaining sugar over 2 slices of brioche. Arrange the mango slices on top and then scatter the shredded mint leaves and remaining blackberries over them. Top with the lids and sprinkle the surface with the rest of the sugar.

3. Toast in a sandwich grill for 2–3 minutes, or according to the manufacturer's instructions, until the bread is golden and crispy. Cut the sandwiches in half and serve immediately with a drizzle of warm coulis, some crème fraîche, sprigs of mint, and a dusting of confectioners' sugar.

TRIPLE CHOCOLATE CHUNK

4 slices of Italian country-style bread
3 oz milk chocolate, chopped
3 oz semisweet chocolate, chopped
3 oz white chocolate, chopped
¼ cup toasted hazelnuts, roughly chopped (optional)

1. Scatter 2 slices of country-style bread with the chocolate chunks and the hazelnuts (if using) and top with the remaining two slices of bread.

2. Toast in a sandwich grill for 2–3 minutes, or according to the manufacturer's instructions, until the bread is golden and toasted and the chocolate is mostly melted. Serve immediately.

Hot Irish Coffee

THIS DELICIOUS CREATION IS LIKE A CROSS BETWEEN A HOT IRISH COFFEE AND A TIRAMISU IN A SANDWICH—PURE LUXURY!

2 tablespoons superfine sugar
¼ cup espresso coffee
2 tablespoons whiskey or Irish coffee-flavored syrup
4 slices of crusty white bread
½ cup chocolate chips
¼ cup mascarpone cheese
cocoa powder, to decorate
lightly whipped cream, to serve

1. Stir the sugar into the hot coffee and mix with the whiskey or Irish coffee-flavored syrup. Dip 2 slices of the crusty bread into the mixture and scatter the chocolate chips over them. Spread the mascarpone over the remaining 2 slices of bread and place them on top of the chocolate chips.

2. Toast in a sandwich grill for 2–3 minutes, or according to the manufacturer's instructions, until the bread is crisp. Dust with cocoa powder and serve immediately with a dollop of lightly whipped cream.

Manchego
AND FIGS

2 thick slices of manchego cheese
2 ripe figs, cut into quarters
4 slices of pumpernickel bread

USE THE BEST POSSIBLE INGREDIENTS IN THIS SIMPLE CHEESE-COURSE DESSERT.

1. Arrange the slices of manchego and the fig quarters on 2 slices of pumpernickel bread and top with the lids.

2. Toast the sandwiches in a sandwich grill for 2–3 minutes, or according to the manufacturer's instructions, until the bread is toasted and the cheese is melting. Serve immediately.

PINEAPPLE AND STICKY
MACADAMIA NUTS

4 pineapple rings in juice, drained
4 slices of panettone
$\frac{1}{3}$ cup mini-marshmallows
$\frac{1}{4}$ cup macadamia nuts, crushed
2 tablespoons vanilla sugar
confectioners' sugar, to serve

DON'T BE FOOLED BY THE GROWN-UP SOUNDING TITLE—THIS IS NOT AN ADULT DESSERT; IT IS STRICTLY FOR THE KIDS AMONG US!

1. Pat the pineapple rings dry on paper towels and arrange them on 2 slices of panettone. Scatter with the marshmallows and crushed macadamia nuts and sprinkle with the vanilla sugar. Top with the remaining two slices of bread.

2. Toast in a sandwich grill for 2–3 minutes, or according to the manufacturer's instructions, until the bread is golden and the marshmallows are beginning to melt. Slice each sandwich into small rectangles and dust with confectioners' sugar. Serve immediately.

CINNAMON,
MASCARPONE, AND AMARETTI

½ cup mascarpone cheese
1 teaspoon ground cinnamon
¼ cup maple syrup
¼ cup Amaretto liqueur
4 slices of panettone
½ cup amaretti cookies, crushed

THE CRUNCH OF AMARETTI COOKIES CONTRASTS PERFECTLY WITH THE SILKY SMOOTHNESS OF THE SWEET CINNAMON MASCARPONE IN THIS RECIPE.

1. Thoroughly mix together the mascarpone, cinnamon, maple syrup, and the liqueur. Spread over 2 slices of panettone, scatter the crushed cookies over it and then top with the remaining slices of panettone.

2. Toast in a sandwich grill for 2–3 minutes, or according to the manufacturer's instructions, until the bread is toasted and the filling is beginning to ooze from the sides. Serve immediately.

JORDAN ALMOND
AND CLOTTED CREAM

3½ oz marzipan, chopped
4 dessert crêpes
¾ cup Jordan almonds, crushed

To serve
clotted cream
honey
lemon juice

1. Scatter the chopped marzipan over half of each crêpe and then sprinkle with the crushed Jordan almonds.

2. Fold the crêpes in half and in half again and toast in a sandwich grill for 1–2 minutes, or according to the manufacturer's instructions, until they are hot and the marzipan is melting.

3. Serve immediately topped with a dollop of clotted cream, a drizzle of honey, and a squeeze of lemon juice.

INDEX